Locked In

written and photographed
by
Mia Coulton

For Rhubarb

Danny's Big Adventure #2

Locked In

Published by:
MaryRuth Books, Inc.
18660 Ravenna Road #2
Chagrin Falls, OH 44023
877.834.1105

www.maryruthbooks.com

First Edition
10 9 8 7 6 5 4 3

Library of Congress Control Number: 2006922990

ISBN 978-933624-06-8

© **Mixed Sources**
Product group from well-managed
forests, controlled sources and
recycled wood or fiber
www.fsc.org Cert no. SW-COC-001530
FSC © 1996 Forest Stewardship Council

Contents

Danny's Yard

Danny loved his yard.

He loved the white fence

that kept him safe.

He loved the tree

that gave him shade

when it was hot.

Danny just loved his yard.

One morning Danny woke up

and looked out his window.

The sun was shining.

It was a beautiful sunny morning.

"I will go out and play

in my yard," Danny thought.

He could hardly wait.

He hurried with his breakfast

then hurried outside.

Danny saw his ball and said to himself, "I will play ball today."

Danny played ball for a long time.

Then he stopped running
and stopped playing ball.
He loved playing ball but it
was not fun playing by himself.

"Maybe there will be somebody
to play with me at the playground,"
Danny thought.
"I love playing with the boys and
girls at the playground."

So Danny said good-bye

to the white fence

that kept him safe.

He said good-bye to the tree

that gave him shade when it was

hot. And off he went

to the playground.

The Playground

Danny ran as fast as he could
when he saw all the boys
and girls.

It was morning recess
and everybody was outside
playing and having fun.

Two girls grabbed hands and started to run to Danny, shouting, "It's Danny! It's Danny!"

"Let's catch him!

Run!

Everybody run and catch Danny,"

they all yelled.

The boys and girls loved playing

chase with Danny.

Danny loved playing chase, too.

One boy almost caught Danny.

Ring! Ring! Ring!

All the children ran

to the school door.

They lined up and walked

inside the school.

Recess was over.

It was time for Danny

to go home.

He had so much fun running and

playing. It made him very happy

and very tired.

Saturday

The next day was Saturday.

Dad always made pancakes

for breakfast on Saturday.

Boy, did Danny love his pancakes!

After breakfast Dad said,

"I have to do some laundry today.

Want to help, Danny?"

Danny shook his head,

"NO."

So Dad went down to the

basement to do the laundry.

Danny went outside

to play in his yard.

He saw his ball.

He ran to his ball.

Then Danny stopped.

He remembered the playground.

Oh, what fun he had playing

with all the children.

So off he went to the playground.

When Danny got to the playground

he did not see

any boys and girls.

Nobody was outside

to play with him.

"I bet they are all inside the

school," Danny said to himself.

Danny was determined
to find the children.

He wanted to play chase
with the boys and girls
just like he did the day before.

He wanted to run and run
and run.

Danny saw a door to the school.

It was open just a little.

Danny squeezed and squeezed...

Danny was in!

He was inside the school.

He saw a long hallway.

He saw lots of rooms

off the long hallway.

But he did not see any children.

Danny started to walk

down the long hallway.

He stopped and looked

into the first room.

It was a very little room with

boxes and boxes of books.

But nobody was there.

The second room he looked into

was also small. He saw

computers and he saw chairs.

But nobody was there.

Danny howled,

"Where is everybody?"

The third room he looked into was very large. He walked slowly into the room.

"Click."

The door closed behind him.

He looked around the room.

He saw lots of desks.

Danny counted twenty desks.

He counted twenty chairs, too.

He saw numbers and letters and pictures all over the walls.

But nobody was there.

Danny started to play

with the letters.

He made a word

with the letters.

c a t

All of a sudden, Danny got

a funny feeling in his stomach.

It was that nervous and jumpy

feeling he got when things just

didn't seem okay.

He realized he was all alone.

He tried to leave the room,

but the door had closed.

Danny tried to push the door

open, but it wouldn't budge.

Danny worried that he was

locked in.

He hurried over to the window.

The window was locked.

He was worried.

He was scared.

He was locked in!

He couldn't find a way out.

"I'm locked in! Help me.

Somebody help me.

I want to go home now,"

Danny cried.

Danny was locked in!

He wanted to be home

in his yard with the white fence

that kept him safe.

He wanted to be under the tree

that gave him shade

when it was hot.

He did not want

to be in the school all alone.

He did not want to be locked in.

Suddenly, he heard a noise.

The knob on the door

began to turn.

Then the door opened.

Dad to the Rescue

Dad was standing at the door.

"Danny, where have you been?"

Dad asked. "I've been looking

all over for you."

"It's a lucky thing I saw the door
to the school was open
or you would have been
locked in all weekend."

"Why did you leave the yard?"
Dad asked. "Were you looking
for somebody to play with
at the school? Today is Saturday
and nobody is at school
on Saturday."

Danny's eyes filled with tears.

He was sorry

he left his yard.

But Dad was the hero for the day.

He rescued Danny!

Danny wagged his tail and smiled.

He began to walk over to Dad.

Then he ran to Dad.

He was so glad Dad rescued him.

Danny began to cover Dad with

licks, almost knocking him over.

Dad gave Danny a pat
on the head and said,
"Let's go home now."

Danny and Dad walked
out of the school
and back home.

Dad went down to the basement to finish the laundry.

Danny went down

to the basement with Dad.

He decided he wanted to help

with the laundry after all.

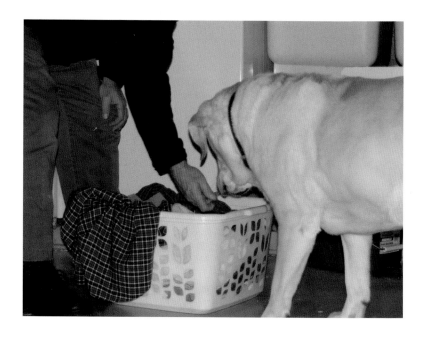